Skill Builders Phonics

by Rosemarie Howard

Welcome to RBP Books' Skill Builders series. Like our Summer Bridge Activities collection, the Skill Builders series is designed to make learning both fun and rewarding.

The Skill Builders Phonics books are based on the premise that mastering language skills builds confidence and enhances a student's entire educational experience. A fundamental factor in learning to read is a strong phonics foundation, beginning with an awareness of the alphabet, understanding phonemic relationships and the concept of words, and moving onto word recognition.

In Phonics Grade 3, readers join SBA kids Matt and Denise on a fun visit to Mystery Mansion, where they learn more about initial and final consonants, vowels, plurals, contractions, possessives, compound words and syllabication, prefixes and suffixes, antonyms and synonyms, and homographs and homophones.

A critical thinking section includes exercises to help develop higher-order thinking skills.

Learning is more effective when approached with an element of fun and enthusiasm—just as most children approach life. That's why the Skill Builders combine entertaining and academically sound exercises with eye-catching graphics and fun themes—to make reviewing basic skills at school or home fun and effective, for both you and your budding scholars.

Table of Contents

Matt and Denise have been invited to attend a birthday party for their friend Opal E. at Mystery Mansion. Mystery Mansion stands alone on a hill in the countryside neighborhood of the town of Reading. The owner, Mr. Ed E (Mr. E, for short), lives there with his wife, Ima E; his son, Abel E; and his daughter, Opal E. They have a dog, two cats, a gray mule, and lots of goldfish in an outdoor pond. The house is surrounded by a large lawn with well-kept gardens. There is a small forest on one side. They have a gardener, Dirt E. Dan; a maid, Eunice; and a cook.

Initial and Final Consonants

C and **s** sometimes make the same sound at the beginning of a word. Choose which letter belongs in each of the blanks in this story about Opal's birthday party.

1. Opal didn't know about the ___urprise party.

2. Everyone in the E's ___ountry neighborhood was invited.

3. Eunice made a ___ake for Opal's birthday party.

4. The ___cent of vanilla filled the kitchen.

5. Eunice went to the ___ellar to get ice.

6. Mrs. E went to the ___ity to buy Opal a present.

7. Opal wanted a microscope so she could look at ___ells.

8. Because Abel can't ___ew, he painted a picture for Opal.

9. Opal's grandmother ___ent her a pearl necklace.

10. Everyone ___eemed to feel like singing.

11. They all ___ang "Happy Birthday" to Opal.

12. Opal was so excited, she turned ___artwheels.

Initial and Final Consonants

Use **g** or **j** to fill in each blank. Then choose five of the words and write a sentence for each, using the word correctly.

1. ____erm

2. ____ail

3. ____eep

4. ____ym

5. ____udge

6. ____ack

7. ____ently

8. ____erk

9. ____ade

10. ____eneral

11. ____eans

12. ____em

Your Sentences:

1. _____

2. _____

3. _____

4. _____

5. _____

Initial and Final Consonants

Use the Word Bank to help find the words using **c**, **s**, **g**, or **j** as the beginning consonant sound in the word search below.

Word Bank

scent
cellar
sell
cell
sent
germ
gem
gently
gym
judge
jerk
jade
jack

z p i g y g t h f z f p
u r l m z c w w l a e t
u a j e e d a j u r c t
z l r s g e m s c e n t
g l e g e n t l y v q f
n e y s c n c e l l k r
k c u y d w t w d j r i
o m m l l e s q e f k p
c r y k v u w r z f l c
x e g v h a k c a j a a
a g f e g d u j l j b b
q w x x v c x b u c t h

Phonics Grade 3—RBP0024

Initial and Final Consonants

Use the Word Bank words ending in **-ck** and the clues below to solve the crossword puzzle.

Across

3. a pack of cards
5. Some people think a four-leaf clover brings this.
7. to be without something
9. You do this before entering a closed door.
10. not healthy

Down

1. a bird that says "quack"
2. left when cars crash
4. very fast
6. the opposite of front
8. close securely with a key

Word Bank

deck

duck

knock

quick

luck

wreck

sick

lack

back

lock

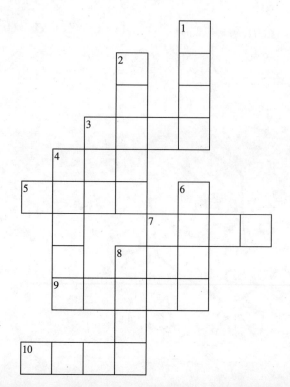

Long and Short Vowel Sounds

Abel E loves the **long a** sound at the beginning of his name. Color the baseballs with the words that contain the long *a* sound; they are some of Abel's favorite things.

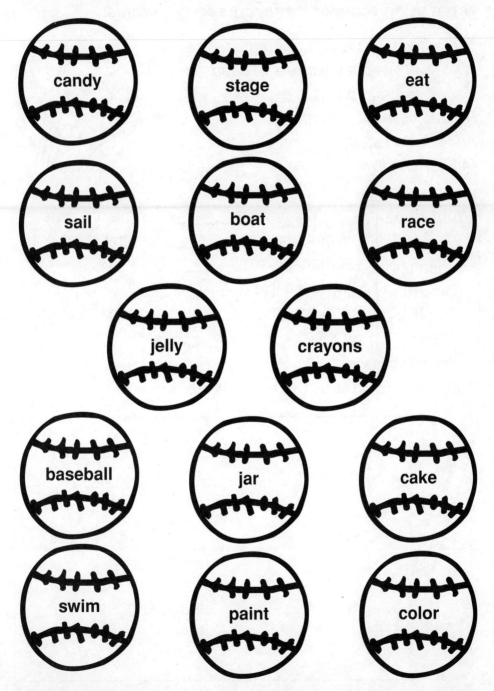

candy

stage

eat

sail

boat

race

jelly

crayons

baseball

jar

cake

swim

paint

color

Phonics Grade 3—RBP0024

Long and Short Vowel Sounds

Mr. E enjoys using words with the **long e** sound. Circle the long e words in the example limerick. Then use the words in the Word Bank to complete the limerick Mr. E wrote using some of his favorite long e words.

There once was a farmer from Leeds
Who swallowed six packets of seeds.
It soon came to pass
He was covered with grass
And couldn't sit down for the weeds.
(Author unknown)

Word Bank

green
bean
believe
see
teeth

You will never _____ me, I'm sure,
When I say that I _____ at my door,
A monster so _____,
He looks like a _____,
And his long _____ are scratching my floor.

Draw the monster in the box below.

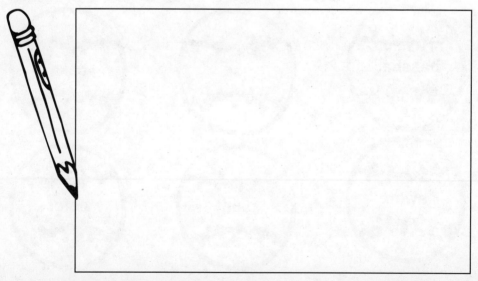

Long and Short Vowel Sounds

Ima's (Mrs. E's) name begins with the **long i** sound, which she thinks is sublime. She loves to work crossword puzzles. Use only the words from the Word Bank with the long *i* sound to work the crossword puzzle below.

Word Bank

sigh	wagon	pink	grow	ground
jog	kites	pie	high	hike
die	jell-o	scream	light	buy

Across

2. Ima makes this sound sometimes when she's sad.

6. the opposite of low

7. Ima watches Abel fly his _____ in the spring.

Down

1. the opposite of dark

3. a long walk on a trail

4. Ima's favorite dessert is apple _____.

5. When Ima forgets to water her plants, they _____.

8. Opal uses a watch to tell _____.

Long and Short Vowel Sounds

Opal E is enchanted with the **long o** sound. She loves to spend time in the kitchen with the cook making doughnuts. Fill in the blanks using only the long o words from the Word Bank.

Word Bank

sunny	do	moaned	Oh	alone
snowy	opened	batter	hot	candy
shut	doughnuts	dough	Well	follow

1. It was a _____ day, and Opal was bored.

2. Opal _____ the kitchen door.

3. "Let's make _____," she said to the cook.

4. "Not again!" _____ the cook. "We just made some on Monday."

5. "Please," begged Opal. "I promise not to throw _____ at the cat again."

6. "_____, all right," said the cook.

7. "Will you let me mix the dough _____ this time?" asked Opal.

8. "If you promise to _____ my instructions," said the cook.

Long and Short Vowel Sounds

Eunice is the maid; her name begins with the **long u** sound. She loves music and living in Mystery Mansion. Use only words from the Word Bank with the long *u* sound to fill in the blanks in this letter. Eunice wrote it to her mother after she started working at Mystery Mansion.

Word Bank

future	music	view	radio	nice
large	scene	huge	mule	stay
cute	goats	horse	ewes	time

Dear Mom,

1. Last week I started working as a maid in a _____ mansion.

2. The _____ from the windows in my room looks out on the gardens.

3. Today I saw some _____ and their lambs eating grass in the field.

4. Mr. E, the owner, has a gray _____ that he rides around the grounds when he wants to think.

5. The cook and I both love to listen to Irish _____ while we work.

6. Abel and Opal, the two children, are both _____ and smart.

7. It looks like my _____ here will be full of fun times.

With love,
Eunice

Long and Short Vowel Sounds

Dirt E. Dan, the gardener, runs into a lot of short vowels sounds while doing his job. Write the words with the short vowel sounds next to the right picture. Circle the short vowel sound(s) in each word.

1. _____

2. _____

3. _____

4. _____

5. _____

6. _____

7. _____

8. _____

9. _____

10. _____

Long and Short Vowel Sounds

This is what happened when Opal and Abel tried to give their dog a bath. Unscramble the words with the **short a** vowel sounds beneath the blank in each sentence. Then write the word in the blank.

1. Opal and Abel decided their dog needed a _____.
thab

2. The dog ran under a _____.
dderla

3. Then he tried to hide in the _____ in the garden.
cksah

4. Finally, Abel was able to _____ the dog by the back of his neck.   **rbag**

5. He and Opal had to _____ the dog to the tub.
rgad

6. Opal began to scrub the dog with a brush, but he jumped out of the tub with a _____.
shrac

7. He ran down the _____ to the woods.
tpha

8. By the time Opal and Able caught him, they were all _____!
mdap

9. They were _____ with mud and grime.   **cklab**

Long and Short Vowel Sounds

Opal and Abel went to the zoo on Saturday. Unscramble the words with the **short e** vowel sounds under each blank. Write the word in the blank.

1. On Saturday Opal and Abel _____ to the zoo.
   ntew

2. Abel took a photo of an _____.
   leehanpt

3. Then he and Opal _____ the animals peanuts.
   def

4. The giraffe's long _____ made Opal smile.
   cken

5. "You can _____ this money to buy ice cream," said Mr. E.   **dneps**

6. The family sat down to _____ and eat their ice cream.   **setr**

7. "Eat it quickly, so it won't _____," said Mrs. E.
   elmt

Long and Short Vowel Sounds

Use the Word Bank words with **short i** sounds to fill in the blanks in the sentences. Then use the words to fill in the crossword puzzle.

Across

2. Abel and Opal were playing by the _____.

4. Opal didn't _____ it was too cold to be swimming.

5. She had a fever and _____.

7. Her mother gave her some warm herbal tea to_____.

Down

1. That night Opal got _____.

3. They watched a _____ float under the bridge.

6. Then they went for a _____.

Word Bank

stick

sick

chills

think

bridge

sip

swim

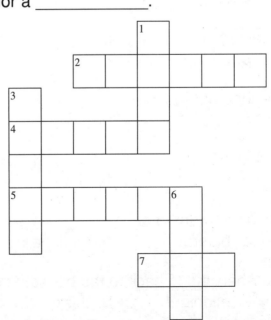

Long and Short Vowel Sounds

In the summer, Abel sometimes helps Dirt E. Dan with the gardening. Choose the word below each blank with the **short u** vowel sound and write it in the blank.

1. Abel found the _____ of a ticket under a rock.
   a. piece   **b.** stub   **c.** part

2. Opal found a lady_____ on a rose leaf.
   a. beetle   **b.** caterpillar   **c.** bug

3. "The soil has too many _____," said Dirt E. Dan.
   a. lumps   **b.** clods   c. thorns

4. Dirt E. Dan has a _____ voice.
   a. loud   **b.** scary   **c.** gruff

5. "_____ that trash in the bag," said Dirt E. Dan.
   a. Stash   **b.** Dump   **c.** Empty

6. The bag dropped with a _____ on Abel's foot.
   a. smack   **b.** screech   **c.** thud

7. Abel sat down on a tree _____ to rub his foot.
   a. stump   **b.** log   **c.** branch

8. He tried not to feel _____.
   a. sad   **b.** glum   **c.** silly

9. A bee began to _____ over his head.
   a. fly   **b.** zoom   **c.** buzz

10. He didn't want to get _____.
    a. bitten   **b.** smashed   **c.** stung

11. So Abel limped back to the house before _____.
    a. midnight   **b.** dusk   **c.** noon

Long and Short Vowel Sounds

Use the short o words in the Word Bank to fill in the blanks in this story about Mr. E's midnight adventure.

<u>Word Bank</u>

wrong	foggy	lock	fox	trot
shock	dog	pond	shot	rob

1. Mr. E told Dirt E. Dan to _____ the chicken coop door.

2. He did not want anyone to _____ his henhouse.

3. What a _____ he had when he found two chickens missing!

4. It was a _____ night, but he wanted to catch the chicken thief.

5. He took his _____, his gun, and his flashlight and walked in the direction of the dark woods.

6. Soon he came to the _____ near the woods.

7. Mr. E thought maybe he was in the _____ place.

8. Suddenly, he saw the gleaming eyes of a _____.

9. He aimed his gun and _____ at the chicken thief.

10. To his disappointment, he saw the fox _____ away.

Long and Short Vowel Sounds

These are some of Opal and Abel's favorite things to eat. Circle the long vowel sounds and put an X on each of the short vowel sounds in each word. Some words may have both long and short vowel sounds in them.

1. strawberry jam

2. milk

3. grapes

4. ice cream

5. green beans

6. rice

7. fish

8. chips

9. peanuts

10. apples

11. beets

12. candy

13. pancakes

14. cheese

Long and Short Vowel Sounds

Mystery Mansion is full of long vowel sounds. Use the words in the Word Bank with long vowel sounds to complete each sentence below.

Word Bank			
gates	smoke	mice	rose
cake	light	paint	green
pave	chime	vase	maid

1. Two stone lions guard the _____ of the mansion.

2. Dirt E. Dan is going to _____ the walks with brick.

3. There is a _____ detector in every room.

4. A computer system monitors the _____ in each room.

5. The grandfather clock in the hall has a loud _____.

6. There are seldom _____ in the mansion because the family has two cats.

7. Mrs. E wants to _____ the living room lavender.

8. She always has a _____ of flowers in every room.

9. Her favorite flower is the _____.

10. Opal wants her bedroom to be repainted _____.

11. Eunice, the _____, enjoys putting puzzles together.

12. Their cook is known for her famous German chocolate _____.

Word Endings

Add the word ending **-ine** or **-out** to the underlined letters in the limericks that Mrs. E helped Abel write. Then write your own limerick using words that end in *-ine* and *-out*.

1. There once was a gray porcup_____,

2. Who decided to d_____ on a v_____.

3. His sn_____ was too st_____

4. To chew on the spr_____,

5. And so he decided to wh_____.

6. Abel was sure that the cook_____

7. Would not be a terrible work_____.

8. He wanted to d_____

9. On fried fish at n_____,

10. But knew nothing ab_____ grilling tr_____.

Word Endings

Opal loves art. She used words that end in **-art** to share what happened at her treasure hunt party. Fill in the blanks with Word Bank words ending in *-art*.

Word Bank

chart	start	part	dwell
quart	tart	depart	cart
yellow	bank	smart	scent

1. One day I decided to _____ a treasure hunt for a party.

2. I thought the woods near the house would be a good place to _____.

3. I made the garden _____ of the treasure hunt.

4. Mom thought it would be _____ to end before dark.

5. The _____ behind the barn was a good place to hide a clue.

6. I put another clue in a _____ jar in the basement.

7. Each person got a cherry _____ after the treasure hunt was over.

8. After we ate the treat, it was time for my guests to _____.

Word Endings

Unscramble the words ending in **-ark** under each blank to read about Abel's afternoon with his friend. Write the word in the blank.

1. My friend _____ came over to play one afternoon.
         larCk

2. He brought his pet _____ with him.
             kraavdrav

3. We went into the _____ behind my house to walk his pet.   **kpra**

4. He wanted to make a _____ on one of the trees.
         arkm

5. Both of us carved our names in the _____ of a big pine tree.   **kbar**

6. We heard a _____ sing as it flew onto one of the tree branches.   **rlak**

7. "We should get home before _____," I said.
          rkad

Word Endings

Use the Word Bank below to help you find the words that end in **-ear** and **-eer** in the word search.

Word Bank

deer	clear	appear	reindeer
steer	gear	smear	pioneer
jeer	spear	shear	

```
i  h  c  a  b  q  n  e  j  p  n  y
v  r  t  t  i  o  h  t  z  c  q  o
p  e  x  u  v  a  p  p  e  a  r  x
r  e  r  e  e  d  n  i  e  r  v  r
e  d  r  j  e  e  r  b  x  z  o  d
m  o  t  g  p  w  a  q  t  i  s  b
g  c  n  r  e  e  n  o  i  p  r  t
m  i  i  r  i  m  e  e  r  a  s  x
m  k  u  e  e  n  v  a  e  x  p  v
s  r  a  e  g  t  h  e  a  e  m
i  i  c  t  j  l  s  b  t  y  a  s
c  e  a  s  c  r  a  e  m  s  r  d
```

Phonics Grade 3—RBP0024

Word Endings

Use the words ending in **-mb** from the Word Bank to work the crossword puzzle.

Across
1. place to bury dead people
2. unable to speak
3. instrument used to untangle hair
4. can't feel
5. hike up a mountain

Down
1. part of your hand
3. small piece of bread
6. a baby sheep

Word Bank

lamb

numb

crumb

tomb

comb

thumb

climb

dumb

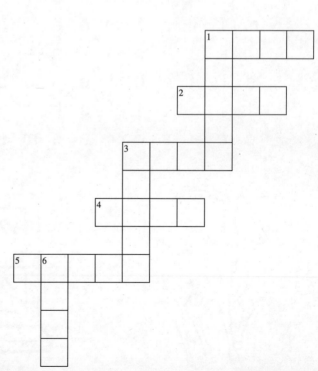

Word Endings

Abel had a narrow escape in the woods near his house one evening. Use the words ending in **-ank** or **-unk** in the Word Bank to fill in the blanks in the sentences below that tell about Abel's adventure.

Word Bank				
slunk	trunk	thank	bank	chunk
blank	rank	chipmunk	skunk	sank

1. Abel saw something moving up the _____ of a nearby tree.

2. He looked closely and saw a little brown _____.

3. He was about to throw a _____ of dirt at the tree trunk.

4. But instead he _____ to his knees to hide behind the tree.

5. He had just seen a _____ walk from behind a bush a few feet away.

6. He froze and his mind went _____.

7. He knew if the animal sprayed him he would smell _____ for days.

8. Finally, he saw the animal turn and walk toward the river_____.

9. "_____ goodness he went the other way!" Able whispered to himself.

10. He _____ quickly out of the woods and went home for supper.

Word Endings

Choose the word ending -oke or -oak to fill in the blanks in the sentences below.

1. "Opal, I'll race you to the big _____ tree," shouted Abel.

2. He started to run as he sp_____.

3. Opal knew Abel was just trying to prov_____ her.

4. She decided to play a j_____ on him.

5. When he reached the tree, Abel yelled, "Opal's a slowp___!"

6. He looked for her, but she had disappeared like sm_____.

7. It was so quiet he could hear a frog cr_____.

8. Suddenly, Abel felt a p_____ in his back that made him jump and yell.

9. When he turned and saw it was Opal, a broad grin br_____ over his face.

10. They both laughed until they thought they would ch_____.

Word Endings

Use the words ending in **-ew**, **-ue**, and **-oo** from the Word Bank to solve the crossword puzzle below.

Across

1. a prompt to help someone who has forgotten their lines
2. the opposite of false
3. liquid you wash your hair with
5. an Australian animal with a pouch
7. water droplets found on plants early in the morning
8. what the wind did yesterday

Down

1. a piece of evidence that helps solve a mystery
2. It means "also."
4. chase after someone or something
6. the opposite of old

Word Bank

new

true

blew

pursue

cue

kangaroo

shampoo

dew

clue

too

Plurals

Draw a line from the singular noun in the left column to its plural in the right column.

1. crayon   clouds

2. pony   feet

3. knife   strawberries

4. lamp   clocks

5. church   butterflies

6. foot   ponies

7. cloud   knives

8. clock   lamps

9. butterfly   crayons

10. strawberry   churches

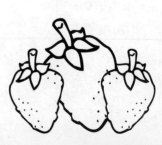

Plurals

Fill in the blanks with the plural form of the words in parentheses to complete the story of Opal's nighttime adventure.

1. Opal went out one night to look at the _____ (star).

2. It was so quiet she heard some _____ (noise) coming from the nearby woods.

3. She turned to look and saw some shining _____ (eye) watching her.

4. Her _____ (foot) froze to the ground.

5. As she stared, into the moonlight hopped a family of _____ (bunny).

6. The _____ (whisker) on their _____ (nose) twitched as they stared back at Opal.

7. Suddenly a series of dog _____ (bark) broke the spell.

8. The family of _____ (rabbit) ran away, and Opal hurried into the house.

Plurals

Find the **plural** form of the singular Word Bank words hidden in the word search below.

> ### Word Bank
> | face | brother | flower | class |
> |------|---------|--------|-------|
> | woman | mouse | berry | library |

```
j f h p y f l o w e r s
q k i o p z g n i s u q
f s r n f c c d e o k e
c e y v c a g x g m a x
q i a b b l c a n z o m
s r w e m a a e g r o w
n a k r r o m s s l h s
j r g r c m i z s b o v
o b m i t c h x m e k l
q i i e i e b w z y s h
s l c s z n i b s g t y
q f e b r o t h e r s u
```

Plurals

The ghosts in Mystery Mansion like to collect things.
Write the plural form of each item the ghosts have
collected on the line next to its picture.

1. _____

2. _____

3. _____

4. _____

5. _____

6. _____

7. _____

8. _____

Contractions

Abel E loves to tease his sister, Opal. Use the contractions in the Word Bank to complete the sentences in the story.

1. "See what _____ found," shouted Abel, waving something in front of Opal's face.

2. "_____ just a stinky old sock," muttered Opal.

3. "_____ it look familiar?" asked Abel.

4. "Wait! _____ one of my favorite socks!" screamed Opal.

5. "_____ giving it to the dog to play with," teased Abel.

6. "_____ be sorry if you do," threatened Opal.

7. "_____ take my chances," laughed Abel as he ran away.

Contractions

The ghosts in Mystery Mansion love contractions because they are words with invisible letters. Make contractions from the following words by making some of the letters disappear and replacing those letters with an apostrophe. Then find the contractions you made in the word search on the next page.

1. that is

_____

2. they will

_____

3. what is

_____

4. he would

_____

5. I will

_____

6. we would

_____

7. she would   _____

8. it is   _____

9. we have   _____

10. I have   _____

Contractions

Find the contractions you made from the words on the previous page in the word search below. (You have to add the apostrophes yourself!)

```
r  g  a  i  s  b  i  l  c  r  f  w
e  k  m  l  v  c  k  l  z  l  r  h
a  a  t  x  t  e  n  i  l  z  b  o
w  c  r  h  s  h  e  d  c  e  h  x
v  e  a  a  m  i  w  t  u  j  u  p
r  t  d  h  q  m  h  h  a  q  z  j
s  m  s  b  h  r  a  e  d  x  j  j
e  m  a  p  j  k  t  y  d  t  r  p
c  r  z  q  j  w  s  l  g  s  t  i
d  n  d  u  l  e  e  l  w  a  d  z
r  k  a  e  g  h  c  v  u  q  l  y
h  b  y  u  h  o  f  l  e  z  y  k
```

Contractions

Draw a line from the contraction to the words it represents.

1. that's   what is

2. what's   we would

3. I'll   you will

4. it's   I have

5. weren't   they will

6. we've   can not

7. you'll   it is

8. he'd   that is

9. I've   we have

10. they'll   were not

11. can't   I will

12. we'd   he would

Possessives

The E family enjoys swimming in their lake each summer. Unscramble the possessive words under each blank. Then write the word in the blank to complete the story.

1. Swimming in _____ private lake is one of the E
      (heirt)
   _____ favorite summer activities.
   (amifly's)

2. "It's time to get _____ swimming suits out for another year,"
   said Mrs. E.   (ruo)

3. "Opal," said Mrs. E, "I think _____ suit from last
                                  (oruy)
   _____ season is too small."
   (eayr's)

4. "Fantastic!" said Opal. "I want one like _____ friend
   _____."   (ym)
   (nAna's)

5. "_____ swimming suit needs to be replaced as
         (bleA's)
   well," said Mrs. E.

6. "Why?" asked Abel. "I like _____ just the way it is."
                                 (inem)

7. "The _____ seat is full of holes," replied Mrs. E.
      (tuis's)

Possessives

Abel likes to go exploring in the nearby woods. Fill in the blanks with the possessive form of the word from the Word Bank to read about his adventure.

<table>
<tr><td colspan="4" align="center"><u>Word Bank</u></td></tr>
<tr><td>my</td><td>rock's</td><td>his</td><td>snake's</td></tr>
<tr><td>Abel's</td><td>its</td><td>sun's</td><td></td></tr>
</table>

1. Abel thumped _____ stick on the dirt path.

2. A snake slithered onto a nearby _____ surface.

3. The _____ skin split.

4. _____ mouth dropped open.

5. The snake left _____ old skin and slid away.

6. The _____ rays made the skin sparkle.

7. "I will take the skin home to show _____ family," said Abel.

Possessives

Write the possessive form of the word groups on the line.

1. the flame belonging to the candle   _____

2. the wings belonging to the butterfly   _____

3. the toy belonging to the cat   _____

4. the candy belonging to Opal   _____

5. the sock belonging to Abel   _____

6. the flute belonging to the maid   _____

7. the leaves belonging to the tree   _____

8. the ring belonging to Mrs. E   _____

9. the pan belonging to the cook   _____

10. the car belonging to Mr. E   _____

Possessives

Work the crossword puzzle using the possessive words in the Word Bank. The apostrophe goes in the space with the letter it follows (example: s').

Across

2. The maid took the _____ apron.
4. Ants ruined the _____ picnic.
7. Mrs. E. threw the _____ old swim suits away.
8. "_____ family loves strawberry pie," said Opal.

Down

1. Abel brushed his _____ mane.
3. The _____ hands both pointed to twelve.
5. "That's _____!" yelled Eunice.
6. "_____ flowers are prettier than yours," said Mr. E.

Word Bank

mine	their	clock's	pony's
our	family's	cook's	children's

Compound Words and Syllabication

Choose words from the Word Bank to create compound words below. Write the word in the blank space. You may use some of the words in the Word Bank more than once.

Word Bank

mate	ball	man	play	game
light	room	story	flake	

1. flash_____

2. basket_____

3. foot_____

4. head_____

5. snow_____

6. corn_____

7. sun_____

8. class_____

9. ball_____

10. police_____

11. _____teller

12. _____book

13. _____mate

14. _____ground

15. street_____

16. post_____

Compound Words and Syllabication

Write the words each pair of pictures represents to make
a compound word on the line next to the pictures.

1. _____

2. _____

3. _____

4. _____

5. _____

6. _____

7. _____

8. _____

Compound Words and Syllabication

Unscramble the compound words under each blank. Then write the word in the blank. Draw a line between the two words that make the compound word.

1. Mrs. E makes sure Abel and Opal have a good
   _____ before they go to school.
   raekbastf

2. When Opal and Abel go to school, they go to different
   _____.
   ssalcoorms

3. _____ at their school wears a uniform.
   veryeodyb

4. They both enjoy listening to _____.
   kofallest

5. Their teacher is an excellent _____.
   torysellert

6. Opal loves to write on the _____ after class.
   hclkarboad

7. She is very good at turning _____.
   tarcheelsw

8. Abel goes to the _____ after school.
   ylapgdounr

9. He plays _____ with his friends.
   asketallbb

10. Abel and Opal are having a _____ of
    the days until summer break.   **ountcnowd**

Prefixes and Suffixes

Eunice, the maid at Mystery Mansion, is always running into the prefix **un-**. Add the prefix *un-* to the underlined words in the sentences below. Then make up four sentences of your own using *un-* words from the story.

1. Mr. E was _____ able to turn on the TV.

2. Eunice discovered it was _____ plugged.

3. Opal needed Eunice's help to _____ buckle her safety helmet.

4. Mrs. E asked Eunice to help her _____ zip her dress.

5. Some of Eunice's favorite poems are written by _____ known poets.

6. "Don't leave the garden gate _____ latched," Eunice reminded Abel.

7. Eunice tries to keep the house from looking _____ tidy.

8. Eunice was so busy, the letter from her mother remained _____ opened until bedtime.

9. Eunice helped Opal _____ button her sweater.

10. Because Eunice loves to help others, she is seldom _____ happy.

Write your sentences here:

11. _____

12. _____

13. _____

14. _____

 Phonics Grade 3—RBP0024

Prefixes and Suffixes

Add the suffix -y to the underlined words in the sentences to make a new word. Then write four sentences of your own using four of the new words you made.

1. It was a <u>rain</u>____ day.

2. Opal was feeling <u>grouch</u>____.

3. She told Abel his socks were <u>dirt</u>____ and <u>smell</u>____.

4. He told her she was too <u>pick</u>____.

5. She told him not to be so <u>nois</u>____.

6. Mrs. E was glad the house was <u>room</u>____.

7. She told Abel and Opal to stop acting <u>craz</u>____.

8. Mrs. E asked Opal and Abel to help her make some <u>chew</u>____ oatmeal cookies.

9. The <u>storm</u>____ day began to get brighter.

10. After supper, they all helped do the <u>dirt</u>____ dishes.

11. Then they ate the cookies by candlelight in the <u>dusk</u>____ kitchen.

12. The <u>gloom</u>____ day ended happily.

Write your sentences here:

13. _____

14. _____

15. _____

16. _____

Prefixes and Suffixes

Add the suffix **-er** to each of the words below. Then
write a sentence using the word correctly. You may need
to add a letter or take one away to add the suffix.

1. swim___ _____

2. dive___ _____

3. write___ _____

4. hike___ _____

5. spell___ _____

6. play___ _____

7. paint___ _____

8. read___ _____

9. garden___ _____

10. bike___ _____

Prefixes and Suffixes

Some of Mr. E's favorite words are opposites ending in the suffix **-er**. Use the Word Bank to find all of the *-er* words in the word search below.

```
e  j  b  v  a  l  j  r  j  t  r  e
m  r  i  v  u  r  e  v  q  s  e  u
y  y  e  b  d  t  e  h  f  l  t  r
u  u  p  i  h  y  e  k  n  o  s  e
j  p  g  g  t  a  n  s  a  w  a  g
m  i  i  l  v  t  t  v  g  e  f  r
s  l  t  i  i  r  e  g  b  r  w  a
c  s  e  h  o  e  h  r  r  d  p  l
v  r  i  n  u  n  r  v  p  u  k  u
c  h  g  c  p  s  m  a  l  l  e  r
m  e  k  s  o  f  t  e  r  v  e  k
r  h  x  h  n  r  e  d  u  o  l  w
```

Prefixes and Suffixes

Circle the suffix and prefix in the bold words. Some words may have only a suffix. Other words may have both a suffix and a prefix. Then use four of the bold words in a sentence of your own.

Opal's Apparition

Opal had a **sensation**
She was under **observation**.
But her friends all said,
"It's just your **imagination**!"

But Opal **persisted**;
She really **insisted**.
In spite of the fact,
Her claim was **resisted**.

Then a ghostly **appearance**
Caused a major **disturbance**—
Until the truth was **discovered**
When Able was **uncovered**!

Write your sentences here:

1. _____

2. _____

3. _____

4. _____

Prefixes and Suffixes

The E family often finds themselves doing things over. Write the prefix **re-** in front of each word in the Word Bank. Then use the words to work the crossword puzzle on the next page.

Word Bank

___seal   ___tell   ___print   ___charge   ___fill
___paint   ___place   ___write   ___string   ___make

1. Abel will _____ the story for the family.

2. Eunice wanted to _____ her room.

3. Able had to _____ his bed.

4. Opal had to _____ her story.

5. Mr. E wanted to _____ his book after all the copies were sold.

6. Dirt E. Dan had to _____ the battery on the tractor.

7. Mrs. E asked Eunice to _____ her glass with juice.

8. It would be impossible to _____ the broken vase.

9. Mr. E wanted to _____ the package of popcorn after he had eaten some.

10. Abel wanted to _____ his guitar because the strings were broken.

Prefixes and Suffixes

Solve the crossword puzzle using the **re-** words in the sentences on the previous page.

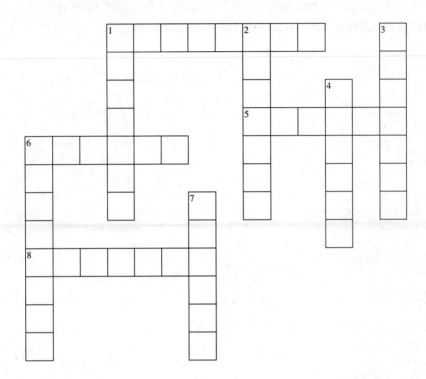

Across

1. sentence 6
5. sentence 9
6. sentence 7
8. sentence 2

Down

1. sentence 4
2. sentence 5
3. sentence 8
4. sentence 3
6. sentence 10
7. sentence 1

Prefixes and Suffixes

Use these prefixes to create new words from the ones listed: **dis-**, **re-**, **un-**, **bi-**, and **pre-**. There may be more than one right answer. Then choose five of the new words and use them correctly in a sentence.

1. ___trust

2. ___charge

3. ___zip

4. ___cycle

5. ___like

6. ___unite

7. ___able

8. ___view

9. ___place

10. ___wrap

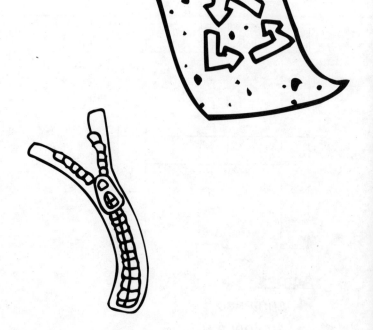

Write your sentences here.

11. _____

12. _____

13. _____

14. _____

15. _____

Antonyms

Mystery Mansion is full of opposites. Draw a line from the word in the left column to the word with the opposite meaning in the right column.

1. shout	enemy
2. up	rough
3. begin	smile
4. noise	day
5. gentle	down
6. friend	peace
7. beautiful	whisper
8. frown	end
9. night	ugly
10. war	silence

Antonyms

Fill in the blank with the opposite of the word in bold type. Use the words in the matching game on the previous page.

1. The maid was going upstairs late at **night**, instead of during the _____.

2. A **smile** was on the maid's face, not a _____.

3. A **whisper** seemed to float by her, perhaps the echo of a _____.

4. She felt a **gentle** tap, not a _____ tap, on her shoulder.

5. Her **beautiful** daydream was ruined when she saw the _____ face of a ghost appear before her.

6. Before she could do anything, the ghost whispered, "Don't scream! I'm your **friend**, not your _____."

7. She almost fell **down** in a faint, but she somehow managed to remain standing _____.

8. Then the ghost disappeared. The maid wanted the night to **end**, not _____ again.

Antonyms

Mr. E knows that Dirt E. Dan, the gardener, will always do the opposite of what he says. Fill in the blanks with the word that means the opposite of what Mr. E said. Use words from the Word Bank.

Word Bank

finish   work   day   gentle   best

1. "Dirt E. Dan, would you start planting the pansies today?" asked Mr. E. Dirt E. Dan should _____ planting the pansies today.

2. "Tomorrow I'd like you to play in the herb garden, Dirt E. Dan," said Mr. E. Dirt E. Dan should _____ in the herb garden tomorrow.

3. "Please don't take all night to weed the flowers, Dirt E. Dan," said Mr. E. Dirt E. Dan shouldn't take all _____ to weed the flowers.

4. "You can't be too rough when you trim the roses, Dirt E. Dan," cautioned Mr. E. Dirt E. should be _____ when he trims the roses.

5. "Dirt E. Dan, you are the worst gardener I've ever had," said Mr. E. Mr. E really thinks Dirt E. Dan is the _____ gardener he's ever had.

Antonyms

Color the parts of the flower with antonyms yellow.
Color the rest of the picture any way you like.

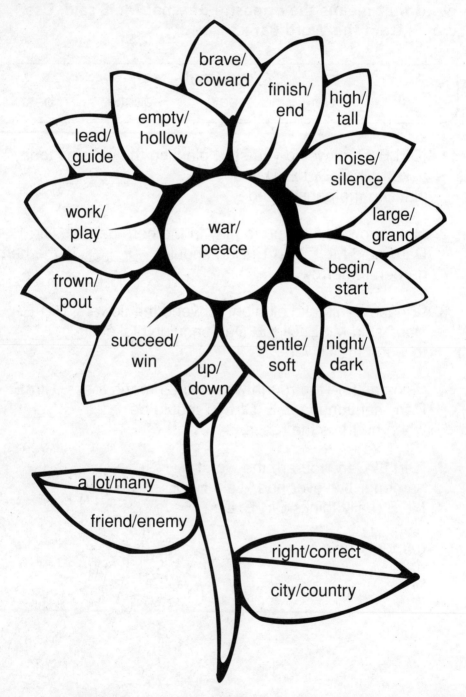

Synonyms

Choose a word from the Word Bank that means the same thing as the word in bold in the sentences below. Use that word to fill in the blank.

Word Bank

forest	purchase	spoil	smell	talk
sunrise	fall	jars	chew	basement

1. Mr. E likes to walk in the **woods** at sunset.
   Mr. E likes to walk in the _____ at sunset.

2. Mrs. E loves walking at **dawn**.
   Mrs. E loves walking at _____.

3. Sometimes Mr. and Mrs. E walk together so they can **chat**.
   Sometimes Mr. and Mrs. E walk together so they can _____.

4. The E family stores food in their **cellar**.
   The E family stores food in their _____.

5. The cellar is cool, so the food doesn't **rot**.
   The cellar is cool, so the food doesn't _____.

6. There are **bottles** of applesauce on the shelves.
   There are _____ of applesauce on the shelves.

7. Opal and Abel carve jack-o-lanterns in the **autumn**.
   Opal and Abel carve jack-o-lanterns in the _____.

8. They don't **buy** the pumpkins; they grow them in their garden.
   They don't _____ the pumpkins; they grow them in their garden.

9. Abel loves to **munch** on licorice.
   Abel loves to _____ on licorice.

10. Opal's favorite **scent** is chocolate.
    Opal's favorite _____ is chocolate.

Synonyms

Draw a line from the word in the left column to its synonym in the right column.

1. flower		road
2. power		dozen
3. story		mob
4. tore		injure
5. clock		cost
6. twelve		blossom
7. street		tale
8. price		energy
9. tomb		ripped
10. smile		watch
11. hurt		grave
12. crowd		grin

Synonyms

Find synonyms of the Word Bank words in the word search below.

Word Bank

neat	fail	loyal	sick
frown	drama	small	piece

```
a  p  g  q  u  j  f  d
j  u  t  l  t  u  a  y
l  i  t  t  l  e  i  d
k  a  k  w  l  k  t  i
n  d  m  p  w  p  h  t
u  y  w  l  o  i  f  r
l  a  t  a  c  l  u  a
f  n  w  y  s  l  l  p
```

Synonyms

Choose the synonym of the word in bold from the three words following each sentence. Circle it.

1. Eating right helps you stay **healthy**.
   a. sick **b.** well **c.** tall

2. A good breakfast gives you **energy** to start the day.
   a. power **b.** vitamins **c.** muscles

3. The E family often enjoys **flapjacks** for breakfast.
   a. French toast **b.** cereal **c.** pancakes

4. Sometimes they eat a **dozen** scrambled eggs as well.
   a. ten **b.** two **c.** twelve

5. Eunice **places** a glass of orange juice by each person's plate.
   a. spills **b.** puts **c.** drops

6. Mrs. E. always puts a vase of **blossoms** on the table.
   a. flowers **b.** willows **c.** wild grass

7. Opal does not think eating chocolate for breakfast is **strange**.
   a. silly **b.** fun **c.** odd

8. Opal offered a **chunk** of chocolate to her dad for breakfast.
   a. sip **b.** bird **c.** piece

9. He **declined**.
   a. stopped **b.** refused **c.** swallowed

10. That made Opal **grin**.
   a. grimace **b.** pucker **c.** smile

Homographs

Solve the crossword puzzle using the homographs.
Homographs are words that are spelled the same but
have different meanings. Each word in the Word Bank
will be used two times.

Word Bank

lead

dove

row

note

object

project

Across

2. a fight

4. a science fair assignment

5. a written reminder to do something

6. a thing

7. the part of a pencil you write with

9. to strongly disagree

Down

1. He _____ into the water.

3. what you do with an oar in a boat

4. a ventriloquist does this with his voice

5. a musician plays these symbols

7. what the student at the front of the line should do

8. a bird used as a symbol of peace

Homographs

Match the picture with the correct homograph. Use the words in the Word Bank. You will use each word two times.

Word Bank

tear   lead   sow   bat   watch   puzzle

1. _____

2. _____

3. _____

4. _____

5. _____

6. _____

7. _____

8. _____

9. _____

10. _____

11. _____

12. _____

Homographs

Write the correct homograph in each sentence using words from the Word Bank. Each word will be used two times.

Word Bank

produce   minute   tear   wind

1. Abel and Opal took the fresh _____ into the house and then went outside to fly their new kite.

2. The _____ lifted the kite high into the air.

3. The kite looked like a _____ speck high in the sky.

4. Abel began to _____ the string around a dowel.

5. The kite had been in the sky only a _____ before the string became tangled in a tree.

6. "It is easier to cut the kite string than to _____ it," said Opal.

7. Opal waited for Abel to _____ some scissors to cut the string.

8. Then she let the kite go without shedding a
_____.

Homographs

Unscramble the homographs beneath each blank. Write the word in the blank.

1. Opal's best friend sits behind her in the same _____
   orw

2. She wanted to write her friend a _____.
   toen

3. Opal's pencil _____ broke.
   elad

4. Her teacher might _____ if she asked to sharpen her pencil.   **jbecto**

5. She looked at her _____. It was almost lunchtime.
   tachw

6. It was her turn to _____ the line for lunch.
   eadl

7. She didn't want to cause a _____ with the teacher.
   wor

8. So she decided to _____ for a chance to talk to her friend at recess.   **chtaw**

Homophones

Circle the homophone in bold that belongs in each sentence. Homophones are words that sound the same but have different meanings.

1. One **night/knight** Abel woke up.

2. It was an **our/hour** before midnight.

3. Sounds seemed to come from the **mane/main** stairway.

4. As quietly as possible he **made/maid** his way to the bedroom door.

5. His legs felt **week/weak**.

6. He carefully opened the door **so/sew** he wouldn't make a noise.

7. The **sent/scent** of a burning candle wafted into his bedroom.

8. He **new/knew** a burning candle could be dangerous.

9. **Which/Witch** room was the smell coming from?

10. A **whole/hole** minute went by.

11. Then he **heard/herd** laughter drifting up the stairs from the kitchen.

12. At once he realized his **ant/aunt** had just arrived and was having a late night snack by candlelight with his parents.

Homophones

Mrs. E loves to write limericks. Use the Word Bank to fill in the blanks in the two limericks she has written. Then find their homophones in the word search on the next page. (Clue: They will be the words you don't use in the limericks.)

Word Bank

knight	made	dear	pear	so	dew
night	rode	deer	hole	sew	
maid	road	pair	whole	do	

1. There once was a _____ very brave,

2. Who set out a fair _____ to save.

3. He _____ far and near

4. To rescue his _____.

5. The _____ met at last in a cave.

6. There once was a frog, _____ they say,

7. Who stayed in a _____ all the day.

8. But when it was _____,
   He hopped out in delight,

9. And sang, "_____ come and join me in play!"

Homophones

Find the homophones of the words you used to fill in the blanks on the previous page in the word search below.

```
r  t  d  c  x  q  u  k  i  u  a  p
q  p  m  z  m  n  q  y  j  q  e  g
d  k  n  i  g  h  t  z  a  s  s  b
u  s  y  d  p  w  s  p  b  d  d  t
z  p  f  e  i  e  d  a  o  r  h  g
l  q  a  w  g  s  u  p  q  g  t  b
h  r  p  s  z  d  s  h  i  e  d  r
o  w  g  v  g  e  p  n  i  d  v  j
m  x  y  s  h  y  l  g  m  a  f  d
y  e  h  k  o  a  r  o  e  m  a  e
r  p  x  z  i  g  f  m  h  x  a  e
u  w  w  o  v  a  i  k  n  w  d  r
```

Homophones

Draw a line from the word in the left column to its homophone in the right column.

1. sun		due
2. heard		mane
3. soar		by
4. waste		tale
5. mail		herd
6. dew		cent
7. knot		no
8. scent		sore
9. main		son
10. buy		not
11. know		waist
12. tail		male

Antonyms

Search through your favorite magazine or newspaper to find the antonyms (opposites) of these words and count how many times you find them. The weather, sports, and arts sections would be good places to look.

1. peace _____

2. dark _____

3. sunrise _____

4. high _____

5. bad _____

6. today _____

7. country (meaning: rural) _____

8. friend _____

9. finish _____

10. old _____

Long Vowels

List ten objects in your house that have long vowel sounds in them. Circle the long vowel sounds. Then write a story using those words.

Example: knife, robe

1. _____

2. _____

3. _____

4. _____

5. _____

6. _____

7. _____

8. _____

9. _____

10. _____

Short Vowels

List ten items out-of-doors in your neighborhood that contain short vowel sounds. Circle the short vowel sounds. Then write a story using the words.

Example: gr(a)ss f(e)nce

1. _____
2. _____
3. _____
4. _____
5. _____
6. _____
7. _____
8. _____
9. _____
10. _____

Word Endings

A limerick is a poem that has five lines. Lines one, two, and five rhyme and contain eight syllables each. The third and fourth lines rhyme with each other and contain five syllables each. Look at the examples on page 62 in the section on homophones. Try writing your own limerick using words ending in **-oke**, **-oak**, **-are**, **-air**, and **-ear**. Practice writing in cursive.

1. _____

2. _____

3. _____

4. _____

5. _____

1. _____

2. _____

3. _____

4. _____

5. _____

Puzzler

1. Write the antonym of *die*. _____

2. Write the homograph of the answer to #1 _____

3. Change the first letter to *h*. _____

4. Now change the first letter to *d*. _____

5. Add the suffix *-er*. _____

6. Draw a picture below of the word you ended up with.

Word Endings

When you go to the grocery store with your mom or dad, make a list of ten words ending with **-k, -ke, -ck, -st,** or **-er**. Show your list to one of your parents.

My Word List

1. _____
2. _____
3. _____
4. _____
5. _____

6. _____
7. _____
8. _____
9. _____
10. _____

C and S Sounds

When you are traveling somewhere, play this game with whomever is riding with you. See who can find the most words on billboards that start with **hard c**, **soft c**, and **s** sounds. Keep track of the words on the lines below. Show your list to one of your parents.

1. _____

2. _____

3. _____

4. _____

5. _____

6. _____

7. _____

8. _____

9. _____

10. _____

11. _____

12. _____

13. _____

14. _____

15. _____

16. _____

17. _____

18. _____

19. _____

20. _____

Prefixes and Suffixes

Make as many words as you can using the base words listed below and the following prefixes and suffixes:
un-, dis-, re-, -y, -ily, -ly, -ed, -ing, -able.

1. desire _____

2. read _____

3. quiet _____

4. cover _____

5. excite _____

6. friend _____

7. happy _____

8. finish _____

9. chew _____

Answer Pages

Page 1
1. s   2. c   3. c   4. s   5. c
6. c   7. c   8. s   9. s   10. s
11. s   12. c

Page 2
1. g   2. j   3. j   4. g   5. j
6. j   7. g   8. j   9. j   10. g
11. j   12. g

Page 3
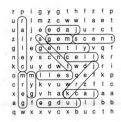

Page 4

Page 5
Long "a" words:

cake   paint   sail   baseball
stage   crayons race

Page 6
Words to be circled:
Leeds   seeds   weeds
Fill in the blank:
believe   see   green   bean   teeth

Page 7
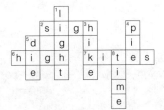

Page 8
1. snowy   2. opened   3. doughnuts
4. moaned   5. dough   6. Oh
7. alone   8. follow

Page 9
1. huge   2. view   3. ewes
4. mule   5. music   6. cute
7. future

Page 10
1. pot (*o* is circled)
2. eggplant (*e* and *a* are circled)
3. radish (*a* and *i* are circled)
4. strawberry (*a* and *e* are circled)
5. melon (*e* and *o* are circled)
6. apple (*a* is circled)
7. pumpkin (*u* and *i* are circled)
8. rock (*o* is circled)
9. frog (*o* is circled)
10. bug (*u* is circled)

Page 11
1. bath   2. ladder   3. shack
4. grab   5. drag   6. crash
7. path   8. damp   9. black

Page 12
1. went   2. elephant   3. fed
4. neck   5. spend   6. rest
7. melt

Page 13
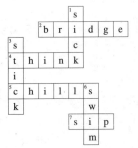

Page 14
1. stub   2. bug   3. lumps
4. gruff   5. Dump   6. thud
7. stump   8. glum   9. buzz
10. stung   11. dusk

Phonics Grade 3—RBP0024

Answer Pages

Page 15
1. lock   2. rob   3. shock
4. foggy   5. dog   6. pond
7. wrong   8. fox   9. shot
10. trot

Page 16
1. Vowels with X: *a, e, a*
2. Vowel with X: *i*
3. Circled vowel: *a*
4. Circled vowels: *i, ea*
5. Circled vowels: *ee, ea*
6. Circled vowel: *i*
7. Vowel with X: *i*
8. Vowel with X. *i*
9. Circled vowel: *ea* Vowel with X: *u*
10. Vowel with X: *a*
11. Circled vowel: *ee*
12. Vowel with X: *a* Circled vowel: *y*
13. Vowel with X: *a* Circled vowel: *a*
14. Circled vowel: *ee*

Page 17
1. gates   2. pave   3. smoke
4. light   5. chime   6. mice
7. paint   8. vase   9. rose
10. green 11. maid   12. cake

Page 18
1. -ine   2. -ine, -ine   3. -out, -out
4. -out   5. -ine   6. -out
7. -out   8. -ine   9. -ine
10. -out, -out

Page 19
1. chart   2. start   3. part
4. smart   5. cart   6. quart
7. tart   8. depart

Page 20
1. Clark   2. aardvark   3. park
4. mark   5. bark   6. lark
7. dark

Page 21

Page 22
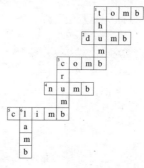

Page 23
1. trunk   2. chipmunk   3. chunk
4. sank   5. skunk   6. blank
7. rank   8. bank   9. Thank
10. slunk

Page 24
1. oak   2. -oke   3. -oke   4. -oke
5. -oke   6. -oke   7. -oak   8. -oke
9. -oke   10. -oke

Page 25
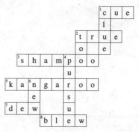

Page 26
1. crayon—crayons   2. pony—ponies
3. knife—knives   4. lamp—lamps

Answer Pages

5. church—churches   6. foot—feet
7. cloud—clouds   8. clock—clocks
9. butterfly—butterflies
10. strawberry—strawberries

Page 27
1. stars   2. noises
3. eyes   4. feet
5. bunnies   6. whiskers, noses
7. barks   8. rabbits

Page 28

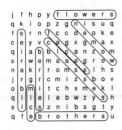

Page 29
1. plates   2. candles   3. socks
4. pennies   5. watches   6. spoons
7. toasters   8. shoes

Page 30
1. I've   2. It's   3. Doesn't
4. That's   5. I'm   6. You'll
7. I'll

Page 31
1. that's   2. they'll   3. what's
4. he'd   5. I'll   6. we'd
7. she'd   8. it's   9. we've
10. I've

Page 32

Page 33
1. that's—that is   2. what's—what is

3. I'll—I will   4. it's—it is
5. weren't—were not   6. we've—we have
7. you'll—you will   8. he'd—he would
9. I've—I have   10. they'll—they will
11. can't—can not   12. we'd—we would

Page 34
1. their, family's   2. our
3. your, year's   4. my, Anna's
5. Abel's   6. mine
7. suit's

Page 35
1. his   2. rock's   3. snake's
4. Abel's   5. its   6. sun's
7. my

Page 36
1. the candle's flame
2. the butterfly's wings
3. the cat's toy   4. Opal's candy
5. Abel's sock   6. the maid's flute
7. the tree's leaves   8. Mrs. E's ring
9. the cook's pan   10. Mr. E's car

Page 37

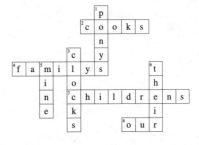

Page 38
1. flashlight   2. basketball
3. football   4. headlight
5. snowflake   6. cornflake
7. sunlight   8. classmate
9. ballroom   10. policeman
11. storyteller   12. storybook
13. playmate or roommate
14. playground   15. streetlight
16. postman

Page 39
1. streetlight   2. midnight

Answer Pages

3. chalkboard
5. toothpaste
7. butterfly

4. grasshopper
6. sunglasses
8. mouthwash

Page 40

1. break-fast
3. every-body
5. story-teller
7. cart-wheels
9. basket-ball

2. class-rooms
4. folk-tales
6. chalk-board
8. play-ground
10. count-down

Page 41

1. unable
3. unbuckle
5. unknown
7. untidy
9. unbutton

2. unplugged
4. unzip
6. unlatched
8. unopened
10. unhappy

Page 42

1. rainy 2. grouchy 3. dirty, smelly
4. picky 5. noisy 6. roomy
7. crazy 8. chewy 9. stormy
10. dirty 11. dusky 12. gloomy

Page 43

1. swimmer 2. diver 3. writer
4. hiker 5. speller 6. player
7. painter 8. reader 9. gardener
10. biker

Page 44

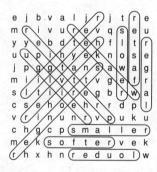

Page 45

Line 1. *ation* is circled
Line 2. *ation* is circled
Line 3. none
Line 4. *ation* is circled

Line 5. *ed* is circled
Line 6. *ed* is circled
Line 7. none
Line 8. *ed* is circled
Line 9. *ance* is circled
Line 10. *ance* is circled
Line 11. *ed* is circled
Line 12. *un* and *ed* are circled

Page 46

1. retell 2. repaint 3. remake
4. rewrite 5. reprint 6. recharge
7. refill 8. replace 9. reseal
10. restring

Page 47

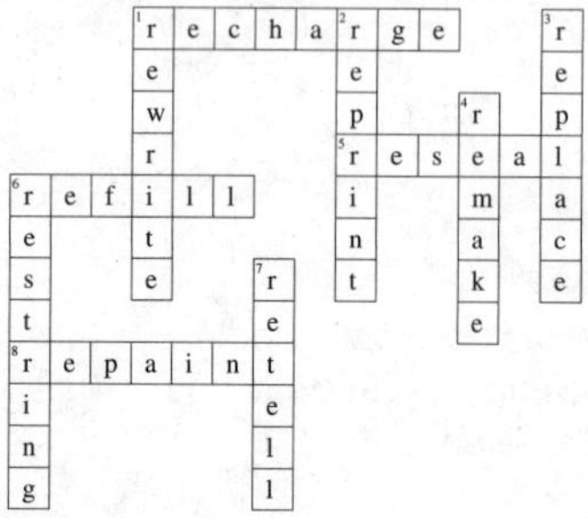

(crossword puzzle with answers: recharge, refill, repaint, reseal, rewrites, etc.)

Page 48

1. dis- 2. dis-, re- 3. un-, re-
4. bi-, re- 5. un-, dis- 6. re-
7. un-, dis- 8. pre- 9. re-, dis-
10. un-, re-

Page 49

1. shout—whisper 2. up—down
3. begin—end 4. noise—silence
5. gentle—rough 6. friend—enemy
7. beautiful—ugly 8. frown—smile
9. night—day 10. war—peace

Page 50

1. day 2. frown 3. shout
4. rough 5. ugly 6. enemy
7. up 8. begin

Page 51

1. finish 2. work 3. day
4. gentle 5. best

Answer Pages

Page 52

The antonyms, which should be colored yellow, are

up/down   work/play   noise/silence
city/country   friend/enemy
war/peace   brave/coward

Page 53
1. forest
2. sunrise
3. talk
4. basement
5. spoil
6. jars
7. fall
8. purchase
9. chew
10. smell

Page 54
1. flower—blossom
2. power—energy
3. story—tale
4. tore—ripped
5. clock—watch
6. twelve—dozen
7. street—road
8. price—cost
9. tomb—grave
10. smile—grin
11. hurt—injure
12. crowd—mob

Page 55

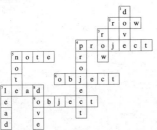

Page 56
1. b. well
2. a. power
3. c. pancakes
4. c. twelve
5. b. puts
6. a. flowers
7. c. odd
8. c. piece
9. b. refused
10. c. smile

Page 57

Page 58
1. bat
2. lead
3. puzzle
4. sow
5. watch
6. bat
7. tear
8. puzzle
9. tear
10. sow
11. watch
12. lead

Page 59
1. produce
2. wind
3. minute
4. wind
5. minute
6. tear
7. produce
8. tear

Page 60
1. row
2. note
3. lead
4. object
5. watch
6. lead
7. row
8. watch

Page 61
1. night
2. hour
3. main
4. made
5. weak
6. so
7. scent
8. knew
9. Which
10. whole
11. heard
12. aunt

Page 62
1. knight
2. maid
3. rode
4. dear
5. pair
6. so
7. hole
8. night
9. Do

Page 63

Page 64
1. sun—son
2. heard—herd
3. soar—sore
4. waste—waist
5. mail—male
6. dew—due
7. knot—not
8. scent—cent
9. main—mane
10. buy—by
11. know—no
12. tail—tale

Answer Pages

Page 65
The words you are looking for in the magazine or newspaper are:
1. war   2. light   3. sunset
4. low   5. good   6. tomorrow
7. city   8. enemy   9. begin
10. new

Page 66 (Answers will vary.)
Here are ideas to help you think:

sofa	ceiling	iron
keys	table	light
plate	people	

Page 67 (Answers will vary.)
Here are ideas to help you think:

car	step	plants
children	bird	robin

Page 68 (Answers will vary.)
Here are word ideas to help you start thinking:

joke	broke	choke
croak	soak	care
bare	dare	fare
hare	fair	stair
lair	dear	near
fear	tear	bear
snare	share	

Page 69
1. live   2. live   3. hive   4. dive
5. diver   6. Draw a picture of a diver.

Page 70 (Answers will vary.)
Here are some ideas if you are having trouble thinking of words:

sack	rack	check
toothpick	snack	

Page 71 (Answers will vary.)
Here are some possibilities:

city	save	care
call	car	seven

Page 72
1. desire
desirable

2. read
readable

desired
desiring
undesirable

unreadable
reading
reread
ready
readily

3. quiet
quietly
quieted
quieting
disquiet

4. cover
covered
covering
uncovered
recovered
recover
uncover

5. excite
excited
excitable
exciting
excitedly
unexcited

6. friend
friendly
unfriendly

7. happy
happily
unhappy

8. finish
finished
unfinished
finishing
refinish
refinished
refinishing

9. chew
chewy
chewable
unchewable
rechew
chewed
rechewed